OUTSI

"Catherine Pritchard Childress crafts her vision on a grand canvas, creating Biblical and ancient historical settings that feel as alive and urgent as the scenes that take place in modern-day Appalachia. *Outside the Frame* is a book of women's voices, some singing, some crying, and some raging at cruel fate, all of them searching for 'evidence/that we stood together in paradise.' These poems pursue the truths that transcend time and place, that bind us together in the experiences of love, heartache, and attunement that matter most in life. I rarely have read a new volume of poetry that moves me as much as this one does, a book that makes me immediately think of other poets I need to share it with, how I will teach it in my classes, and what I can learn from it to enlarge my own work. *Outside the Frame* may be a debut collection of poems, but Pritchard Childress ingrains it with the wisdom and heart of many lifetimes closely studied, deeply felt, and masterfully rendered. Once read, these wonderful poems will not be forgotten."

— JESSE GRAVES, author of *Merciful Days*

❧

"'Out beyond ideas of wrongdoing and rightdoing, there is a field. I'll meet you there,' says Rumi. So the poems in *Outside the Frame* find rhythms of care and judgement. Catherine Pritchard Childress sings them into women's songs, humans' songs, bound to place and tradition, but not to time. These are songs of attention. She gathers them here for release."

— LEAH NAOMI GREEN, author of *The More Extravagant Feast*

❧

"While many of these poems are set explicitly in the Appalachian South, it is terrain that Plath or Sexton would recognize. With humor, sensitivity, and sometimes rage, Pritchard Childress transforms old (and young) wives' tales into a volume of lyrical lives of domestically marginalized saints and s(p)inners."

— MARIA DAHVANA HEADLEY, author of *Beowulf: A New Translation*

❧

"*Outside the Frame* is a compelling accounting of the life of a woman bursting from her skin, pushing back against constant attempts at restraint, at expectations that inhibit her. Pritchard Childress' beautiful, smart poems give a vivid, lyrical accounting of lives of women of her own generation as well as ages past, so complicated by the complex cultural and religious milieu they inhabit, interspersed with a consideration of the heart maps of many prominent women of the Bible. These poems are not angry, cynical, sneering, or petty; the voice is wise and very generous. But the message is very clear: she will not become a 'roadside field burned to dry dust' by this world, and the world is better for it."

— RITA SIMS QUILLEN, author of *Some Notes You Hold*

"At once polished, wild, and bewitching, this provocative collection reads like a stack of saved secret letters. Here, Catherine Pritchard Childress has drawn back the curtains of the inner sanctums of the religious South and borne witness to the extraordinary complexity, the largess, of ostensibly small lives. These poems disrupt, they trouble patriarchal waters, and they ask two things: What really happens to women who dissent, and are you strong enough to wonder?"

— SHAWNA KAY RODENBERG, author of *Kin: A Memoir*

"What I love in this collection is the intersection of home and belief, of innocence and experience. The poems in *Outside the Frame* stray between wound and wonder, observed from the "cloister" of the Blue Ridge where the speaker is at once a child and a mother, where persona and the personal are intertwined in the confrontation of trauma and beauty. Hymns and rock'n'roll are equally sacred in these poems as Pritchard Childress turns her ear toward the music found in the everyday of family and in the myths that sustain us. Ultimately, these poems complicate the notion of rurality as simple or isolated and offer up a wish to bind each of us, 'Let pared heart bear no bruise nor scar.'"

— MATTHEW WIMBERLEY, author of *Daniel Boone's Window*

Outside the Frame

POEMS

Catherine Pritchard Childress

Outside the Frame

Catherine Pritchard Childress

© 2023

All Rights Reserved.

POETRY

ISBN   978-1-958094-26-6

BOOK & COVER DESIGN   EK LARKEN

COVER IMAGE   PAULA MORIN *[UNSPLASH]*

EastOver Press encourages the use of our publications in educational settings.
For questions about educational discounts, contact us online:
www.EastOverPress.com or info@EastOverPress.com.

PUBLISHED IN THE UNITED STATES OF AMERICA BY

EASTOVER
— PRESS —
ROCHESTER, MASSACHUSETTS
www.EastOverPress.com

Outside the Frame

"Fool," said my muse to me,
"look in thy heart and write."

Sir Philip Sidney

CONTENTS

I

II

III

I

Putting Up Corn

In August, he places a bushel bag at my feet,
bursting with pride at the sweet corn he brings
from the rusty bed of an old man's truck.
Three dollars a dozen will cost me
eight hours. Shucking, silking, washing, cutting,
cooking what could be bought
from the freezer section where I find
green beans our mothers would plant,
pick, cook, and can, planning
for hard winter which might not come,
hungry children who would.

I peel back rough, green husks to reveal
so many teeth that need brushing, smiling
knowing smiles because he has delivered
my submission.

I strip silk with a small brush,
turning each ear over in my hand,
rosary said to the blessed mother
whose purity he thinks I lack.

Our Father who art in Heaven, I didn't do the dishes today.
Hail Mary, full of grace, I don't own an iron.
Glory be to the Father, I speak my mind.
Hail Holy Queen, I called for takeout again.

I cut each kernel loose with a sharp blade,
shave away what I believe in, what he would change,
scrape the cob and my soul clean,
leaving nothing behind.

I place a dozen gallon bags at his feet,
bursting with my sweet-corn yield,
in a kitchen where I don't belong, planning
for hard winter which might not come,
hungry children who will.

Made as reparation for being
the woman I am, placed in a freezer
where each time a bag is removed
he will be reminded that once, in August,
I was the wife he wished for.

Leah's Aubade

I know I am not the one you bargained for,
not the one you labored in fields
for seven years to marry. I am the wasted
bride price, the one who came to you veiled
in my father's deceit, pretending to be the woman
who will dutifully tend your sheep,
carry water from the well where you first fell
in love with Rachel, whose kiss made you cry.

This morning shines on bitter tears
glowing in the aftermath of your surprise.
Too drunk last night to notice whose bed you shared,
to sense my body's subtleties, discern my cries,
you waken to the wrong life, find me
good enough to share your bed, bear your sons,
but not enough to keep you from the fields
haggling, again, for a wife.

Wife to Wife

My father admonished me
to remember you.
He couldn't have known
how I would heed
his warning. I don't
condemn your trespass,
I commend you,
don't blame you
for wanting to stay
behind in a place
where you had friends,
unstained clothes,
a name.
I imagine your skeptical exit
from the gates of Sodom,
walking toward your life,
the view stinging
your eyes like desert sand.
A clouded image of Lot,
who didn't fill your needs,
but satisfied his greed
when he pitched his tents.
Looking back was better
than blindly following
a father who offered
your daughters' virtue,
kept his honor
locked behind doors,
conspired with angels
who lauded his intentions,
grieved his union
with an impure wife.
My father warned me
of the wrath
that changed you
to a pillar, scattered you

throughout that razed city,
but he didn't know you
were the one
with power to cleanse,
couldn't fathom teaching me
to remember
just how much you are worth.

Down Elk

We stood beside Elk River
as often as the Good Lord allowed.
Women teetered on rocky banks,
swaying in high heels as they sang
"Shall We Gather at the River."

Men traded their polished wingtips
for waders and the Joy, Joy, Joy, Joy
down in their hearts that could come
only from dunking a fellow believer
beneath the frigid water.

While the old-timers led the new convert
to the preacher who'd led them to the Lord,
my brother and I beckoned other kids
to join as we edged closer and closer
to the swirling, saving water.

Our Sunday shoes were wet
when we bowed our heads to pray,
but when Daddy raised his King James
high in the air and baptized this his brother
or that his sister in the name of the Father,
the Son, and the Holy Ghost, we paid
attention. We paid respect to our father
and the Son who paid for our sins.
We watched with wonder
as the water washed clean,
and when the sinner Daddy submerged,
emerged a soaking-wet saint,
tears streamed down my face.

Sunrise Service

Easter Sunday, still dark morning,
Creedence Clearwater Revival booming
insurrection across the hall at parents
shamed by daughters singing "Bad Moon Rising,"
dancing in satin underwear, twisting hot
rollers into each other's hair.

Frocked in robin's egg, violet, daffodil
Mom purchased at Hill's, we retaliate
with bare legs, big hair, and black eyeliner
heated to a white-hot point with the tiny Bic
I kept between cellophane and soft pack
of Marlboro Lights.

Smoke ascends from the window, masked
in clouds of White Rain, Secret, Love's Baby Soft,
perfuming the sloped roof where summer
will find us oiled in Johnson's and iodine,
careful to hide budding breasts, triangled in bikinis,
from our father's eternal glare.

Knowing the end is coming soon,
we belt out the last verse, buckle sandals,
tie sashes, tiptoe to church in twilight
to celebrate the resurrection, certain
that nothing will rise but the sun.

Blossoming Indigo

I coveted the Wranglers my brother wore
when we played outside, durable denim
seat impervious to rocks, sticks, glass shards
unearthed when we scooted toward the stream,
worn knees grass-dyed lucent chartreuse,
pockets deep enough to hold his morning finds—
bumboozers, bottlecaps, buckeyes—treasure
I had to secure in the dirty hem of my skirt—
what "ladies" wore to church, to play, to school
where other girls arrived each September
in Lees with pleats and pink pinstripes.
But they're pink! My rebuttal when my father
defended his edict with Deuteronomy 22:5,
declared jeans are for boys, refused
even my plea to try on one pair, just to see,
to take on each lean leg like I'd watched
my friends do, ease them over calves, knees,
shimmy past thighs, hips, around my waist;
look over my shoulder; discover curves
blossoming indigo; a woman in the glass
reflecting why he always said no.

Ascending

She heard her girlhood in the creaking ninth stair—
the top of the steep ascent to a room
she shared with her sister, and brother too
after the paneled partition was positioned,
then the thin, voile curtain suspended
to veil the view between his bed and hers
where she would lie awake nights—

sometimes listening to a DJ's late-night voice
counting down the Top 40 or taking requests
while she waited, primed to push "RECORD"
on the cassette deck if she heard "Urgent,"
"Angel of the Morning," or "Jessie's Girl."

Sometimes singing along with George Jones
and her brother as he belted "Yesterday's Wine"
into a hairbrush, never missing a word, note, or cue—
one song in the set he performed each week.

Sometimes (when he'd sneak Sara past their parents)
hearing the muffled moans of what passed as lovemaking,
scratch of denim yanked from skinny hips,
loose change and lip gloss falling to the hardwood floor,
the giggle of faux protest, whispers of touching
beneath t-shirts and a pink lace bra, hands
inching down ribs and navels, just inside
waistbands, lingering on the edge of that final step.

Polysemy

My mother is a two-story Victorian
restored to original, then rented
to a family of five.

A concrete goose,
dressed in seasonal sweaters,
waving from the front porch,

store signs that read
God Don't Like Ugly.
Bait. Knives. Jesus Is Coming.

Sometimes my mother is a cloistering maple
hiding heaping hulls of pop-up campers
and littered yards just beyond the bridge.

Sometimes Tootsie Rolls or gospel tracts
thrown from beds of pick-ups, tractors,
vintage convertibles, and from horseback.

Tent Revivals. Youth Revivals.
The full bloom of Rhododendron
and Decoration Day graves in June.

She's the web of ridges that thread
every holler to every creek—
Dark, Sugar, Sinking, Roaring . . .

A five-a.m. mountaintop sunrise
heaping the sky with dish, dish, dish
of banana pudding, peach cobbler, creamsicle fudge.

Mostly, she's a roadside field burned
to dry dust with a promise
that Echinacea, asters, and yarrow will thrive.

Queen Mother

When I stepped from the scalding water onto my roof,
I knew you would make me queen, would watch the Mikveh
wash me pure, ready for the seed your smile promised.

I didn't know you would ordain Uriah's death, that your god
would smite our firstborn son (retribution for the so-called sin
that made me finally your wife, secured my place in the bed

where I conceived a king, watched you die) but not before
I contrived your last wish, removed Adonijah from his throne,
his mother from my palace, secured my place in the legacy,

made Solomon your heir. Our fourth son, not our first
whose birthright was usurped by whom Jeremiah calls
your son, twenty-eight generations removed,

King of the Jews, descendant of my tainted line.

Bathsheba's Bath

I was aware of your leering
when I dropped my robe,
dipped one foot into the tub,
eased my calf inch by blistering inch,
testing the waters to see
if my friends were right
about the way you look at me
when I walk into a room
with the man who defends your crown.

It was no accident you were there
that day taking in the view
from your palace roof
or that I moved into sight
just in time to see
the corners of your mouth
curl to invitation.
Response bubbled past my thighs
as I slipped deeper into the heat.

Charm

When he quipped "It's colder than a witch's tit,"
I knew he had never kneaded his woman's breasts.
Didn't press poultice of cabbage leaves to ease
engorgement of useless milk after each blue babe
she bore, didn't bind her with bandages—winding

       winding

              winding

an incantation to the edge of her breath. I know
he did not rest his hand in her back's small
while she heaved grief.
            He did not loose her,

release the fire,

release her pain.

Instead of You

I buried the wild oats,
ones I'd sown with you
on the wrong side of a bar,
in the wrong bed,
deep in the dark, familiar, soil of home.

Covered them over
with a patchwork quilt
pulled from a chest
filled with every hope except my own.
Forgot them

when I wore Mama's white lace,
set a farmhouse table
with Wedgewood china
and three highchairs,
made supper, made love, put away dishes,

put down roots
with a boy who was raised right,
right here
in this place where I returned
when I left you by the murky water

you loved so much
though I never knew why
before we held hands on the pier
then plunged to the secret bottom,
our toes in sultry mud,

tangled legs and hearts
moved by a current
too strong for a hidden cove
and a sheltered girl,
lying bare beside you

and the water we shared.
Holding hands, we said
good-bye
to a possibility
that wouldn't be veiled in white,

where sometimes I return
and dig deep in the mire
to exhume a desire
that can't be contained in a cedar box
at the foot of this wrong bed.

Solo

That summer, I earned my keep
singing Saturday nights in a bar,

serving Pabst on tap between sets
of Lorrie Morgan and Sammi Smith's

"Help Me Make It Through the Night,"
requested at least three times each week

by Tim, who taught me the two-step
after hours, circling the concrete floor,

a soaring raptor, sizing up prey,
holding me closer than the steps called for.

Still reeling, I followed his lead
to a seedy motel. His quickquick, slow,

slow rhythm, mastered on the dance floor,
pulsed long after his misstep in bed,

where I cradled him in my arms,
softly singing him to sleep.

II

Salome's Ghazal

I left my veils in the laps of men for whom I danced,
'Round their necks, wrists—in this silken costume, I danced.

At the birthday celebration befitting a lascivious king—
Planned by my mother, a gift for her groom, I danced.

Your guests witnessed you pledge your solemn oath
To grant my wish, so in your reception room, I danced.

Terracotta firelight flickered off my jeweled breasts,
Kindling improper desire—perfumed, I danced.

Thinking of John who spurned my incessant advances,
Swaying to the suggestion of his coming doom, I danced.

Gratified by my performance, you promised to make good.
To sate the desire that leaves me consumed, I danced.

Reluctantly you delivered his head on a bloody tray,
Dressed his body, buried him, and at his tomb, I danced.

Oeuvre

A real boyfriend would've cared
I was only twelve, still jailbait,
never had a slow, wet, kiss, mouth
full of wrestling tongues, never
found my G-spot or knew
I had one, that his plans
for the backseat would wound
more than a pink crescent
between baby-fat thighs,
the thin layer of dignity
I cleaved to with zeal of backwoods
religion sacrificed for a few quick,
dry strokes—would've offered
a rag for the blood, comfort in his arms,
not his chest heaving against me
again and again
pounding out his body of work.

Sustenance

The passed-down silver serving fork pierced
ground beef, egg yolks, tomato sauce,
delaying the inevitable meeting between
Mother's seasoned hands and supper.

I burned to lace my fingers with hers,
knead the bowl's flavored flesh
with scarred knuckles, feel albumen slip
through fingertips like a housewife's dream,
bind the pieces with leftover crumbs.

She palmed the mixture into an oval loaf,
keeping the mess for herself. I readied the pan,
set five Dresden places while she rinsed
the egg-white glaze from her wedding ring,
watching its luster wash down the drain.

Housewife's Howl

after Allen Ginsberg's "Howl"

I watched the strongest woman I'd known crumbled by convention. Exhausted cotton shift dragged down narrow, hardwood stairs at rooster-crow to satisfy a hungry family. Coal-eyed babies drained her clean as the patterned linoleum she mopped in moonlight. She submitted per the instruction of the Apostle Paul to a head-of-household husband whose heart was filled with arteries wasted by the gold-flake biscuits and sausage gravy he demanded even when he knew it would kill him—staggering her with the burden of children, checkbook, and chopped wood that wouldn't burn if it was too green, too wet, or from a willow tree. Lessons a city-coddled girl had no use for meant survival in the blue mountain home of a woman who bared her body to a long-haul trucker after she jumped from her Daddy's window bound for South Carolina and a marriage license; who poured powdered formula, and pints of liquor down the drain every time he promised to quit; who praised the Lord when he found Jesus, and followed, three babies in tow, to build a church and a life—to be a pastor's wife who gave to the poorer, prayed for the lost, witnessed to backsliders, comforted the sick, spent her life washing clothes and smart-mouths out with soap, cleaning up our house and our acts, serving meals, serving others, serving God, teaching accidental lessons to a daughter bound to put right the heart of this woman she hoped never to become.

Sarah

I only wanted Hagar to bear my son.
How could I have known she would love
My husband, that when I asked him
To send her and Ishmael away, his face
Would reveal he loved her too,
That I was right when I guessed
He was in her bed (long after she conceived),
That he was thinking of her
When he hummed in the fields,
When I caught his distracted gaze,
When he kissed me goodnight.

My barren body cannot compete
With the thrill he must feel
When the soft curves of her youth
Respond again and again to his touch,
Cannot elicit his body's firm response
With only the light pressure of an ankle
Against his calf, the brush of a hand
On his forearm, a probing tongue—
Cannot bear to see his eyes follow her
As she braids her hair, nurses their son,
Cannot watch her become my husband's wife.

Concubine

Sarah told me I should be happy
I am the one
whose pleasure comes without condition,
the one who folds into your arms for a moment of release,
whose body still responds to your bidding,
giving you your first, if not favored, son.

She told me I should be happy
I am not the one
who folds your linens into stacked squares,
plucks the field's debris from your beard,
not the one who lathers your pubic hair into her own
with shared soap, is stirred by your sleep sounds,
that yours is not the first face I see each day.

She told me I should be happy,
                               which is easy for her to say.

Traveler's Chapel

Last stop before we pressed our faces against
the Buick's tinted glass hoping to be the first
to see waves peeking from gaps in the skyline.
The walk from foyer to altar came natural,
our feet programmed by three services
each week in our father's country church.

In this tiny, roadside chapel we scribbled
names in the Guest Book alongside vacationers
from Atlanta, Raleigh, Columbia, black stars on a map,
far from the Blue Ridge Mountains that cloistered us,
save for one week each year when grandparents
treated us to summer vacation at Myrtle Beach.

We crowded into Mimi's green Electra—
drying tears, blowing kisses, promising
to attend church on Sunday, the only condition
attached to our reprieve, a promise my mother's
mother found little reason to keep.
We rolled into the chapel's gravel lot
thirty miles from total immersion.

Sure our sin would find us out, we tithed
spending money in the chapel's donation cup,
then I posed on the front step, a sibling on either side,
faces fixed on the camera's lens, evidence
that we stood together in paradise.

Down the Bank

Red dirt held a promise that mattered
to a girl and boy digging for night-crawlers
with sticks, and spoons snuck from the drawer
where Mama thought her Mr. Goodbars were hidden,

or hoarding crusty-lipped RC bottles plundered
from neighbor's trash and roadside ditches
to swap for shiny dimes to spend on Cokes
and two-cent bubble gum at Hughes's Store

where cats slept near the blade set to cut thick
slices of bologna, and where inability to back down
from a big brother's dare pulled me
down the candy aisle to fill my pudgy hands with treats
I wouldn't pay for but knew I should.

The weight of dirty pockets measured the trip
across the plank bridge towards home,
where the brother I adored waited
to receive his portion of the spoils, to give
approval I longed for but didn't deserve.

Red dirt held a promise that mattered to a girl
home-grown on the Ten Commandments,
the Golden Rule, and a black leather belt
with a glowering brass buckle, used liberally
by strong hands—a lesson in each lick.

Hush

I parked beside a winding mountain road
to gather Black-Eyed Susans for Mom
and courage to round the next bend—a sharp left
onto my father's farm where I once hid
in the hayloft with Jason Martin, taking turns
reciting poems, safe from the ridicule of real men.
Those lost afternoons buried a secret deeper
in me than the paperbacks tucked beneath
tawny bales, the one I'd come to tell Dad now.
He wants me to marry a nice girl, punch a timecard,
ssshhh crying babies while the woman gets supper.
Wishing, for his sake, I wanted that too
will provide little comfort when I see his face
in my rear-view mirror, broken after I've laid bare
a future that began with whispering in his barn.

The Chastening

The long-winded preacher said you were taken,
that God will let one stray only so far, but once you cross
His invisible line, He will decide enough is enough,
take you out of this world so you cannot continue
to dishonor his Holy name or that of our God-fearing father,
dead too, though by natural causes (he was right with the Lord).

He cautioned your friends who came to pay their respects,
"This will be your price," theatrically gesturing
to the yellow roses that blanketed your casket, for carrying on
with their NASCAR watching and beer drinking on Sunday
afternoon, instead of joining spirit-filled saints who made laps
around padded pews, stopping occasionally to shake a hand,

hug a neck—just like a six-year-old stranger wrapped tiny fingers
around yours so you could lift her from the burning car,
heeding your instruction to hold on tight so well, you had to pry
her hands loose from your dark, coarse hair, shove her back
through an open window when you looked over your shoulder
and saw the tractor-trailer that struck you down.

Sunday School

Sunday morning and I am washed in nothing
more than light, heat, and guilt
planted deep by my father's voice, saying,
Get up! We go to church on Sunday morning.
Not to races, not to ballgames, not to the beach.

Still, I dig my feet into the white powder,
keeping time with the tide and their heads,
two dark like my own, one a sun-kissed mystery,
bobbing like bottled notes on foamy peaks,
free from clip-on ties, patent leather, and tradition.

Sunday morning and I worship at an altar
where my winter whitewash goes golden,
foolish children build houses upon the sand
never knowing, as I once learned in a hymn,
that the house on the sand went splat.

Capriccio

Through the kitchen window I see ropes
swinging from the maple's arthritic limb
then the lengthening fingers of the maestro
conducting her strings in a concerto,
each grip cueing another turn that spirals her,
summer-knotted hair skimming the grass,
upturned face scored by sun and leaf-shadow,
bare feet raised toward the whirling cord
that winds *ritardando* to a breathtaking end.

Pedicure

When I asked for red, he motioned to a palette
of nail polish—*Dutch Tulips, California Raspberry,
Malaga Wine, An Affair in Red Square.* My only task
to choose—to decide what this man will stroke
on my canvases when I lie back into the bulky arms
of his chair, slip my small feet into a burning basin, surrender
to his skilled hands, versed in exposing tender layers.
I offer him ankle, calf, shallow impression behind my knee,
barely hear his exotic chatter while he kneads away pain
of late nights spent at the kitchen sink, throb
of high heels striking sidewalk and stairs. I nestle deep
into his strong arms as lithe fingers smooth neglect,
nurture muscle, flesh, render feeling full to my fiery toes.

III

Other

"... There were also women looking on from a distance,
among whom was Mary Magdalene"

Mark 15:40

Your chosen men returned
to their homes, their nets,
their doubts. Could not watch you
force final, shallow breaths
into your lungs, bearing down
on the same feet I wet with tears,
wiped clean with my hair,
muscle and flesh tearing away
as you cried out to your Father.

I wiped your mother's tears,
listened to you offer
forgiveness to the thieves
beside you, waited to hear you
call my name, prayed you could see
me there, not forsaking you,
not betraying you, not leaving
you, but longing for you
to finally acknowledge me.

You beheld her and your beloved
John before you died, but I was left
to follow your cold body,
stand silent while a stranger held you
in his arms, sheathed you in silk
and perfume, laid you in a dark tomb.
Still I waited, believing you would come
for me, not leave me, three days
later, crying again at your feet.

The Cinnamon Peeler's Wife

after Michael Ondaatje's "The Cinnamon Peeler"

I am the cinnamon
peeler's wife. Smell me.

Imbued with his seasoned hands,
my feet scatter a fragrant path
signaling his journey started here:

stripping silk stockings
from my thighs, nipping toes,
his spicy fingers floating

above my arched back,
perfuming my pillow
like Solomon's whore
whose scents coaxed
a boy to a lover's bed

like this one
where his palms
met my blades,
seized my shoulders
with an intoxicating grip,

then with one deft motion,
took me, held me
like his kokaththa's handle,
marked me with a lingering scar.

Seduction

I should have realized when he stopped
at the overlook eager to show me the view
of his mountains, his home—to share
not too distant high school memories

of hiding six-packs from his mother.
When he treated me to a buffet lunch,
timidly pushed his food around his plate
while I ate, I should have known—

but I can't remember a man courting me.
Handholding and dinner dates gave way
to the garage and Sports South years ago—
I don't know the last time someone wanted me,

skimmed my jawline with fingertips
traced the hollow above my collarbone,
kissed the freckles on my shoulders one by one,
kneaded the length of my spine, small of my back.

It had been so long, I no longer recognized
the ritual, the moves—couldn't see anything
but a boy who said finally, I spent the summer
learning the notes to your favorite song—

then he played "Dance Me to the End of Love."
I watched his lips purse, then part, in a whispered tune,
his hands move along the length of the guitar's neck,
his fingertips pluck and strum, coaxing a familiar chord.

Sōkhenet

*"... Let us look for a young virgin to serve the king and take care of him.
She can lie beside him so that our lord the king may keep warm."*

I Kings 1:4

Prescribed for my virtue, youth,
promise I can restore this man,
his impotent fields, the kingdom
bound in his vigor. No small task—
its weight bearing down like quilts
heaped high on his withering frame.

So cold he resists wool's comfort
yet finds, in my body, a balm,
respite from sure surrender—
to his wife, his sons,
his deteriorating flesh.
Still, no one body, however

servile, however pure can meet
the needs of a king. Even when
his pulse quickens beneath my touch
I know what those who brought me here—
counselors, physicians, greedy
sons—do not.
        I am not enough.

Elegy for June Cleaver

It took only thirty minutes, once each week
for you to set the bar I try to hurdle
but limbo at best, finding how low I can go.
If not for you, he would never expect a kiss
and cold drink at the door, instead
of juice-box and crying child.
You taught them that six p.m. brings meatloaf,
mashed potatoes, bread from scratch, a lesson
I un-teach with cardboard boxes of pizza.
Thanks to you, the woman of my husband's dreams,
he thinks he married Roseanne.
Patiently, you nurtured Wally and The Beaver,
hosted playdates for boys with funny names
like the ones I call my own boys behind their backs,
over wrinkled laundry that I don't iron.
Finally, you can get some rest
in a hardwood box, polished lemon fresh.
Kick off your heels, while I kick up mine.
Shed those pearls, lose the lipstick.
But be sure not to leave your apron behind.

Even after Dark

after Claudia Emerson's "Pitching Horseshoes"

Never content being my wife, you seek more
in the pages of your books. Offer yourself
to the white sheets you scribble on, then revise,
blotting out any chance for me to hold you.

You spend hours at your grandmother's desk,
between me and the coffee mug you painted
green with red cherries, forever reaching
for what sustains you through all-nighters,

leaving me to slip from your side into the shade
of the oak tree out back, where I built a flowerbed
for the first birthday you celebrated in this house.
Hosta, Impatiens, and Bleeding Hearts submit

to weeds that thrive under your neglect,
roots holding on tight. Your reading lamp glares
from your bedroom window, asserting
your coveted solitude, casting just enough light

for me to see the stakes you drive me to night
after night, trudging the length of the pit,
hoping for a ringer, always adjusting my grip,
deciding when to release, when to hold on.

Wedding Vows

When she stood before God and all those witnesses to say I Do
What she really meant was *I Don't. I Won't.*
She meant *You've got to be kidding me.*
Who wants to spend the rest of her life with some poor, old, sick guy?
What she meant is *I don't intend to wash your clothes or wear lipstick anymore.*
I won't walk barefoot in your kitchen.
I promise to gain at least twenty pounds, to honor my Daddy's name,
and to obey a plethora of self-help books.
She could have meant I Do.
I do have a mind of my own, my own life, friends, musical taste.
I do know how to order take out and maintain separate accounts.
She meant with this ring *I will have a headache, often!*
I will leave the lights on at night so I can read.
I will breathe down your neck and in your face with morning breath.
I will forsake shaving my legs from the knee up
Until Death Do Us Part.

Portrait

I bathed and lotioned you to a pink sheen,
sponged away milk curdled in your folds,
dressed you in starched linen and leather
lace-ups—shoes mailed with coupons clipped
from a Gerber cereal box—to be bronzed
so they could flank the photo your father
waited in the side-yard to capture.

He chose the cushioned rocker to prop you in,
dragged it out beside the fading Shrub Rose—
its blooms so much like my nipples, cracked
as your smacking lips drained my breasts
in twenty-minute intervals. Lullabies, rocking,
each day's routine subject to your rhythm.

He snapped three shots to wind the film.
I posed you in the chair's corner—certain
cherry arms and spindles could not keep you
from toppling heavy-headfirst into overgrown grass—
backed away from his composition, away from you.

Your constant hunger hanging heavy;
his, looming over a four-poster bed.
Your soured spit-up on my shoulder;
his musk between my thighs. Your weight
stretched like every month's last paycheck
across my hips; his, thrust against them.

I didn't tell you I needed my body back
from you—from him, didn't tell you
lullabies are lies (pictures too),
that diamond rings turn brass; glass
breaks; babies fall; bronzed shoes tarnish:
and mothers disappear

                                    just outside the frame.

Beyond the Rope

He pressed his face against canvas
ignoring signs marked "Do Not Touch,"
zooming in, with one bright iris,
on primary colors and shapes.

Shading him from the docent's view,
I guided his fingers with mine
as he brushed the raised acrylic—
oiled red monochrome of apples,
barn, incongruous sails atop
hand-hewn canoes floating downstream
between log cabins and tall pines.

I described windows of churches—
holding his fingertips steady,
traced straight lines of rectangled frames,
sketched curves of intricate stained glass,
leaned in close as he discovered
the rendering of wood and stone.

He asked me to read every word
written beside each vivid scene—
to repeat these lines:
"She's a tree of life to them
who can lay hold upon her,"
wondered why no "she"
appeared in the painted landscape
he could see only when his hands,
held tightly in my own, reached out;
yielded to my pressure; stroked trees,
revealing fruit—his eyes open.

Let Jam Come

after Jane Kenyon's "Let Evening Come"

Let spring's late light
coax berries from the vine—
each day deepening their blush.

Let sun warm her back, soil
cushion her knees as she fills
her tub with fruit. Let jam come.

Let stem and leaf fall away
as the maple's winged seed.
Let pared heart bear no bruise nor scar.

Let sugar draw sweet juice as a woman
pulls her man to her breast. Let heat
clot crimson pulp. Let jam come.

To the lemon that tempers the cloy,
the vessel waiting to be filled, to the sultry
southern air let jam come.

Let it come, as it will, in a blistering bath.
Her labor set, sealed, and shelved.
Let jam come.

Beaver Lodge

Crisscrossed branches rise in a spire,
casting short shadows on the green
water, held tight by weeds and mire
slapped into place each year between

abscission and first frost, heaped
higher when predators,   cold,   snow
threaten to penetrate the stick-steeple
rooted deep in the river below

the bobbing dives of Bufflehead ducks.
They enter this fortress unseen, alone,
shielded by all they have dammed up,
protected by walls hardened to stone.

New

I chose them from a bin in the produce
aisle, sifted through for the tiniest ones,
small enough to cook up without slicing
in two—fingerlings to add to the beef
stew recipe saved for an afternoon
when no stain, book, husband, or child
called my attention away from oil, thyme,
red wine, and flour thickened to a roux;
boneless chuck roast, cut into small cubes,
dredged and browned, flavored with yellow onion
petals, garlic bulbs; ribbed celery hearts,
baby-cut carrots, and new potatoes—
young, delicate, paper-thin skinned, soil-specked
from fresh harvest, evidence of winter's end
wrapped in my hand like a child's prized marble.

Cirrhotic

Sometimes the dead need to hear death's process:

1. *Fluid will accumulate in your abdomen. This can be
   uncomfortable and cause difficulty breathing.* Check.

Sometimes the dead laugh and tell you if you have anything
wonderful to say about them you should say it now, but you only
think of their skinny ankles and calves, the green Hornet they drove
to the pool—your cousins piled inside, even the one who dry-humped
you upstairs when you were eight and believed it was a game.

Sometimes they are lying in living rooms in hospital beds
delivered by Hospice waiting for the doctor's pronouncement;
aware of every pouched micturition, every defecation, conscious
others are too, but too polite to acknowledge the shittiness.

2. *As the liver loses its ability to detoxify, harmful chemicals build
   up in the blood and brain, leading to mental changes.* Check.

3. *As brain function continues to decrease, sleep and confusion will increase.*
   Check.

4. *The doctor may prescribe medications to help maintain comfort and dignity.*

Sometimes the dead think their favorite aqua blouse too ordinary for
burial, that caskets should be open because "people will be curious."
Sometimes they count seconds between abdominal cramps.

5. *In the final days of liver failure, medication will be less useful.* Check

6. "Please God, come take me now." Check.

Pyre

You told me once you were going to paint a coffin,
brush it with bones and flames, like the lizard-skinned
race cars and motorcycles that speed away
from your garage, emblazoned with your name.

Asked me if I would place you in it, put you on display,
bury you in your own creation. So claustrophobic
I can't even be comforted by a down coat on a cold day,
I agreed, only if you promised I would have no coffin at all.

Split the wood, prepare the pyre, shroud me in red,
lay me on a bed of oak, throw the first torch,
kindle the consuming fire, dance in my smoky haze,
wail your grief, surrender my body to the blaze.

Notes

Many of these poems owe a debt to poet and critic Jeannine Hall Gailey who first claimed, "persona poetry creates space for the silent or slandered women in already-known mythologies and folktales" ("Why We Wear Masks: Three Contemporary Women Writers and Their Use of the Persona Poem." *Poemeleon: A Journal of Poetry*).

"Leah's Aubade"
This poem is informed by Genesis 29.

"Wife to Wife"
Lines in this poem echo Luke 17:32 and reimagine Genesis 19.

"Blossoming Indigo"
"The woman shall not wear that which pertaineth unto a man, neither shall a man put on a woman's garment: for all that do so are abomination unto the Lord thy God." Deuteronomy 22:5.

"Polysemy"
With thanks to Aaron Smith. Polysemy refers to "the phenomenon whereby a single word form is associated with two or several related senses." *Oxford Research Encyclopedia of Linguistics*.

"Queen Mother"
This poem is informed by 1 Kings 1 and 2, as well as Matthew 1:1-17 "The Genealogy of Jesus Christ," the only scripture that acknowledges Bathsheba in Jesus's lineage. Even here she is only named as "Uriah's wife."

"Charm"
With thanks to Susan O'Dell Underwood.

"Sarah" and "Concubine"
These poems are revisionist renderings of Genesis 16.

"Salome's Ghazal"
This poem reimagines Mark 6:14-29 and draws inspiration from Oscar Wilde's *Salome*, particularly Aubrey Beardsley's illustrations, *The Stomach Dance* and *The Dancer's Reward*.

"Sōkhenet"
This poem's title refers to Abishag the Shunammite (1 Kings 1) and comes from a root *skn*, "attend to," "take care."

"Cirrhotic"
Some of the numbered steps in this poem are based on information provided in *What Can Be Expected in End-Stage Liver Disease*, Canadian Virtual Hospice.

ACKNOWLEDGMENTS

The author gratefully acknowledges these publications where poems in this collection first appeared, sometimes in slightly different forms and with different titles:

A! Magazine for the Arts: "Elegy for June Cleaver"

Appalachian Review: "Beyond the Rope" and "Blossoming Indigo"

Black Moon Magazine: "Charm" and "Let Jam Come"

The Cape Rock: "Instead of You"

Connecticut Review: "Down Elk"

drafthorse: "Pedicure," "New," "Sustenance," and "Even after Dark"

Kaimana: "Oeuvre"

Kudzu Literary Magazine: "Ascending"

Kudzu Review: "Beaver Lodge"

Louisiana Literature: "Other" and "The Cinnamon Peeler's Wife"

The Mockingbird: "Housewife's Howl" and "Bathsheba's Bath"

North American Review: "Hush"

The Notebook: "Concubine"

Southern Poetry Anthology, Volume VI: Tennessee: "Putting Up Corn"

Southern Poetry Anthology, Volume VII: North Carolina: "Down Elk"

Still: The Journal: "Seduction," "Sunrise Service," "Traveler's Chapel," "Sunday School," "The Chastening," "Portrait," and "Polysemy"

Stoneboat: "Leah's Aubade" and "Solo"

Town Creek Poetry: "Down the Bank"

Women Speak, Volume VIII: "Cirrhotic" and "Capriccio"

With profound and abiding gratitude to Jesse Graves, who showed me *what's at stake*, and Don Johnson, who inspired me to say it better.

ABOUT THE AUTHOR

CATHERINE PRITCHARD CHILDRESS

 lives in the shadow of Roan Mountain in East Tennessee. She teaches writing and literature at Lees-McRae College. Her poems have appeared in *North American Review, The Cape Rock, Louisiana Literature, Connecticut Review, Appalachian Review, Still: The Journal, Stoneboat,* and *drafthorse,* among other journals. Her work has also been anthologized in *The Southern Poetry Anthology,* Volumes VI and VII: Tennessee and North Carolina, and in *Women Speak,* Volumes VII and VIII. She authored the poetry collection *Other* (Finishing Line Press, 2015).

Explore more poetry published by

EASTOVER
— PRESS —
www.EastOverPress.com

Surface Fugue
Ralph Sneeden

❧

Exquisite by September
Shayla Hawkins

❧

The Sins of Sweet Mortality
Marilyn Fox & Nancye McCrary

❧

Crow Funeral
Kate Hanson Foster

❧

The Places That Hold
John Davis Jr.

❧

Midwestern Poet's Incomplete Guide to Symbolism
Erica Anderson Senter

❧

What We Take With Us
Sylvia Woods

❧

The Cutleaf Reader
Established and emerging writers as published in *Cutleaf*,
our literary journal of short stories, essays, and poetry.
(www.CutleafJournal.com)

Printed in the USA
CPSIA information can be obtained
at www.ICGtesting.com
JSHW020306191023
50444JS00006B/36

9 781958 094266